The Little Book of Remedies

A Concise Handbook for the
Lasavia Healing Remedies

Leila Lees

99% Press,

an imprint of Lasavia Publishing Ltd.

Auckland, New Zealand

www.lasaviapublishing.com

Copyright ©Leila Lees, 2021

This book is copyright. Apart from any fair dealing for the purpose of private study, research, criticism or reviews, as permitted under the Copyright Act, no part may be reproduced by any process without the permission of the publishers.

ISBN: 978-1-99-115196-4

Contents

Using the Remedies

Introduction	9
Context and Lineage	10
Mother Tinctures and Stock Bottles	12
Dosage Bottles	13
Looking After Stock Bottles	13
Using Essences	14
How often should I take my remedy?	14
Choosing a remedy	15

The Lasavia Healing Remedies

Weeds

Chickweed	20
Cleavers	22
Comfrey	24
Cress	26
Dandelion	28
Scotch thistle	30

Native Plants

Hangehange, New Zealand Privet	34
Karamū	36
Kōtukutuku, New Zealand Tree Fuchsia	38
Nīkau	40
Pōhuehue	42
Ponga	44

Insects

Bee	48
Cicada, Kihikihi wawā	50
Cricket, Pihareinga	52
Praying Mantis	54
Chinese Paper Wasp	57
Tree Wētā	59

Minerals

Chambered Nautilus	64
Diamond	66
Pearl	68
Pounamu	70
Pyramid Rock, Greywacke	72
Rose Quartz	74

Birds

Huia	78
North Island Kākā	81
Kōtare, New Zealand Kingfisher	84
Sparrow	86
Tūī	89
White-faced Heron, Matuku moana	92

Trauma Blends

Remedy for Connection to Life Force	96
Remedy for Interrupting Negative Thought Patterns	97
Remedy for Shock	98
Trauma Remedy for Children and Childhood	99
Remedy for the Trauma of Illness	100
Remedy for Creating Space to Exist	102

Using the Remedies

Introduction

When I plug into the great cacophony of the modern human world, I find my sense of equilibrium is rocked. I become overwhelmed with the storming upon our natural ecosystem in which we dwell, and as I partake in a myriad of activities, I lend my voice in the cacophony. It is when I step away that I begin to arrive into my inner sensibility. It is how I am brought to stillness by the rapturous melodic sound of the song thrush, or I see the small sharp red berries of the nīkau on the ground scattered by the kererū or the tiny white flower of the chickweed, that I remember the humblest, most beautiful communication is happening beneath my feet, and I am touched. This is why the Lasavia Healing Remedies are important for me.

These remedies were created through an evolution of my personal journey, observations of nature and landscape and study of the flower remedy method. I have a natural sensitivity to the subtle energies and worlds behind the physical, and these remedies embody the complex interweave of land and ecosystem and our relationship to these.

The Lasavia Healing Remedies are vibrational medicines that contain the essence of the plant, animal or mineral for which each is named. The concept of essence refers to the innate quality that is possessed by an object. It is at once an exquisite expression of simplicity, yet also reflects a weave of a complex patterning within nature.

The Lasavia Healing Remedies are created with water and preserved in brandy. They work on the subtle bodies inviting a connection into the healing qualities of nature.

Modern society separates our spiritual interconnectivity from our daily activities. The remedies remind us that this is merely a construct, and sometimes they work by awakening us to how we are living and relating to the world around us.

Over the years, I have created many different remedies. In this small book I introduce six sets of remedies from Aotearoa, New Zealand; wild weeds, native plants, insects, minerals, birds and trauma blends. This book is a brief summary of the meaning of the remedies, how they were made, and how to use them. Those wishing to delve deeper into the subject matter may like to read my forthcoming comprehensive handbook on vibrational remedies: *Essence*.

Context and Lineage

Vibrational medicines were used by indigenous people throughout time and place. Ian White in his book *Bush Flower Essences* describes how the aboriginal people of Australia would eat the flower to obtain the beneficial effects of the plant. 'The essence, in the form of dew made potent by the sun, would thus be consumed with the flower' He describes further how if the flower was inedible they would sit in a clump of flowers to absorb the healing vibration. Paracelus (1493 -1541), alchemist, physician and philosopher, a highly observant man, who worked ceaselessly in his exploration of medicine, collected the dew from flowers to treat health and emotional imbalances in his patients. The collection of dew could have come from his connection to folk lore and his thirteen years of travelling from town to town working as a healer among swiss peasants.

Dr Edward Bach (1886-1936) started as a surgeon and then in 1919 took up a post at the London Homeopathic Hospital and was working in Bacteriology as a pathologist not as a homeopath. He started to prepare vaccines using homeopathic methods and gave a paper proposing that vaccine therapy was closer to homeopathy than allopathic medicine. He saw both homeopathy and allopathic medicine with mutual respect and recognition. Later when he created the vibrational medicines, he is famous for today, he named them remedies. These remedies are now called *Bach Flower Remedies*. He further observed that dew formed in the shade did not carry the same potency as dew formed on flowers in the sun. He drew the conclusions that the sun had the effect of potentising a remedy.

Around the time of my first foray in vibrational medicine I visited a flower remedy practitioner on Waiheke Island who introduced me to Mary Garberly's *The New Perception Essences*. Mary began to create New Zealand remedies in the 1970s. She met with a "farmers wife, Jane," who was making remedies following Dr Bach's method. Mary started using these and then met another woman, Sally, who had made 'many more New Zealand remedies.' This was to lead to the formation of the New Zealand Flower Essence Co-operative.

Mary Garberly was a pioneer in the field of natural health care and flower remedy research in New Zealand. She was born in Titirangi, surrounded by the native forest of the Waitakere ranges. In retrospect she saw that this natural landscape was a place of healing when needed. She created a wide range of essences in New Zealand which she named *New Perception* and traveled throughout New Zealand teaching and empowering others to use them. She saw nature as a loving cooperative partner. Mary Garberly died on February 20th 1998.

I was introduced to remedy making by Oraina Jones who lived in Brightwater, Nelson. Oraina developed a collection of vibrational remedies called *Earthsong*. Oraina and I worked together for a number of years developing a series of remedies that explored the influence of place and time in the potency of the remedy.

Mother Tinctures and Stock Bottles

Remedies are made by transferring the essence of the flower, plant, mineral or animal into water. This is catalyzed by sunlight and effected by other particulars from the environment in which the remedy is made. The water is then preserved in quality brandy of equal proportion to the water. This is called the mother tincture.

From the mother tincture, a stock bottle is made. The stock bottle contains approximately four to eight drops of the mother tincture, preserved in a 50% brandy to water ratio. This is what practitioners use to create dosage bottles of remedies. The mother tincture is not for direct use. Stock, on the other hand, may be taken directly.

Dosage Bottles

A dosage bottle can have a mix of different remedies and is created specifically for an individual's requirement. A dosage bottle is not meant to last for months, it is particular to a person's requirement at the time. At most, there should be 15% brandy to water ratio to preserve for the period the person is taking the remedy. Some people are brandy sensitive. Recovering alcoholics, children and those suffering from candida or other health issues may use apple cider vinegar as a preservative. The dosage bottle should be glass with a glass dropper to prevent the plastic from reacting with the remedy.

Looking After Stock Bottles

The remedy stock bottles have energy and are alive. The energy they contain is robust, but they do need some general care. The brandy can, over time, break down the rubber stoppers; this, in turn, impacts the remedies, so keep them upright. Also, keep them out of the sun – it is best to store them in a cool dark place.

Using remedies

The Lasavia Healing remedies are safe and easy to use. You may prepare a small dosage bottle by mixing 15% brandy or apple cider vinegar with 85% water. Drop 6 to 8 drops from the remedy or the selection of different remedies you wish to use into the dosage bottle to create your dosage bottle. You may also put a few drops of the remedy in your drink bottle or glass of water. You may take them straight from the stock bottle onto your tongue or even onto your skin but take care not to touch your lips, tongue or skin to the glass dropper.

The remedies can be beneficial when rubbed gently on the skin. Places on the body that they can be applied are on the forehead, the soles of the feet, wrists and the palms of the hand. This can be helpful for babies when you are massaging, or also visiting unwell or elderly people. Another way to take the remedies is in a bath. Cleansing and protective remedies can be sprinkled around a room or space, clearing from energies.

How often should I take my remedy?

Sometimes a dosage bottle is for a particular time or crisis. You don't always have to take it until the bottle is finished. Sometimes there is a shift in feelings, energy or circumstance within the first three to four days, so it's a good idea to take the drops regularly at least three times a day for the first three days. A practitioner may give specific instructions as to how long you should take the remedies for and how often. In other cases, remedies may be taken as a 'once-off', as in the case of putting a few drops in a glass of water.

Choosing a remedy

If you are an intuitive person, you may already notice how particular remedies seem to jump out at you. I encourage you to listen to this, pick up the remedy in your hand and sense how it feels before reading about what they do. Another way to choose is to muscle test or use a pendulum.

Muscle testing uses the electrical system of the body to show strength or weakness in regards to a clear question. The body can be a sensitive antenna, but it takes training and listening to your body to pick up the subtle yet strong messages it sends us. When we have a 'yes', the electrical system is strong, so when we muscle test we can resist with strength, pressure that is put in the body. When we experience 'no', the electrical system becomes weakened so it is harder to resist.

One way of muscle testing is to form a circle by touching the pads of the little finger and thumb. With the other hand, touch the pads of your forefinger and thumb and bring this into the centre of the circle formed by the little finger and thumb. Now imagine a strong 'yes' through your body and bring that 'yes' into the circle that you formed with your little finger and thumb. Feel the strength of that and see how that circle stays strong as you try to push it open with the other hand. Next, imagine the 'no' and repeat the exercise with the 'no' – you may experience that the circle is weak and breaks apart more readily. It is always better in learning muscle testing to have someone show you.

Other ways of intuitively testing are to work with a pendulum or a divining rod.

It is good to balance your intuition with your thoughts and inquiries. Please take the time to read about the remedies you have chosen and see whether the information matches what you have been experiencing.

Lasavia Healing does have a set of divining cards and you can use these cards to choose a remedy or decide what will be in your dosage bottle. The other way is to simply read the meanings and see what description resonates for you. If you are choosing for friends or family, it's best to involve them, perhaps asking them which one resonates for them and why.

The Lasavia Healing Remedies

Weeds

Weeds follow human occupation. Weeds have evolved with us. How fitting, therefore, that this range of remedies can effect a potent cure for our various ailments. I feel enriched by my relationship with these plants and in many ways feel their essence bringing me into life. I encourage you to get to know them for yourself, to take a moment to taste the dandelion leaf or place the flower in water to drink or gather the chickweed and the cress for your salads.

Chickweed
Stellaria media

Essence

Protective and nourishing, gives the ability to rest when needed and enables a profound acceptance of oneself, allowing for self-care.

Use

Use in times of transition. It supports a person in the first stages of grief, helping to assimilate a situation that is unexpected or where the circumstances are unforeseen. Chickweed is a good remedy for children and infants, helping them through weaning or when they need support through transitional stages of growth.

Description

Chickweed will be sprawling out, soft, tender and delicious somewhere nearby, particularly in spring and autumn. It prefers to grow in the 'tended' areas of a garden. It has a slightly salty taste that indicates its high mineral content. The leaves of chickweed are oval and grow in opposite pairs. The flowers are small, white and have five petals with deep clefts. The flowers resemble stars with narrow sepals. The fruit are found on elongated drooping stalks and produce tiny yellow-orange seeds.

Meaning

Chickweed is helpful for those who cling to what feels safe even though it is outmoded. It helps us to let go of what is no longer in alignment. Use when stepping out into new work or needing to perform or use technological processes that are unfamiliar. It soothes the nervous system, particularly when it is impacted by a culture of competitive working habits. Rather than be overwhelmed by feelings of inability and not being able to keep up with others, chickweed helps us to realize the contributions we already make, thus emboldening our confidence and self-esteem.

Cleavers
Gallium aparine

Essence

Cleansing and clearing, it enables us to receive the support appropriate for us at any given moment. It opens the ability to reach out to new sources of inspiration.

Use

Helps in uncovering purpose and therefore enables movement in projects that have become stuck. Cleavers are excellent at clearing negative or heavy energies in projects, business, homes and land. Use for dependency and relationships where a person experiences a feeling of being trapped and for despair.

Description

The stems and leaves of cleavers have very fine-hooked bristles, which attach to passing objects, like Velcro. It also fastens itself to adjacent plants or shrubs and grows upwards. Its leaves are narrow, lance-shaped and are rough along the margins and surface. They grow around and along the square and occasionally red-tinged, branching stem. The flowers are white, tiny, and star-like, about 3mm in diameter. It is self-fertilizing and pollinated by beetles and flies. The seeds are round and covered with hooked bristles. As children, we used to call them biddy-bids, and our clothes would often be covered in them. They readily cling to whatever they touch, ensuring dispersal of the seeds.

Meaning

Cleavers seek the light, seek renewal, and seem to cut through all weighty matters. Its lightly anchored root system enables it to let go and move to a new place to grow again. The point between the stem and the leaf is the point of integration. This integration is an acceptance of everything in that moment, exactly how it is. It aids us in identifying and letting go of our old patterns and behaviours, as well as aiding us in reaching out to others when needed. It is helpful in putting in place interdependent partnerships, a reminder that we don't have to be self-reliant in everything.

Comfrey
Symphytum × uplandicum

Essence

Comfrey brings attention to the patterns that help us evolve and also the patterns that may be holding us back. This remedy can act as a bridge allowing for the accessing of old wisdom and the bringing of this into the contemporary.

Use

Use when dealing with anger. It gives the ability to acknowledge and listen to anger that can boil up inside. Through this, we can find constructive ways to communicate what is triggering the anger. Comfrey enables shifts in patterns that are not serving us, particularly patterns of addiction and dependency.

Description

The comfrey that grows in New Zealand is known as Canadian comfrey or wandering comfrey. It differs from *Symphytum officinale* (the comfrey of the old medical apothecaries) in that it is softer, and its flowers have a pinkish tinge to them.

Comfrey is a plant of contrast. Its pink flowers are delicate, charming and floating like pink bell-shaped dresses. The flower unfolds like a concertina. The racemes – the shoots on which they grow – are botanically described as scorpioid because they curve like a scorpion's tail. The leaves are prolific, large, and grow as part of the hairy stem.

Comfrey supports and aids the knitting of fractures and broken bones from its effect on the soft connective tissues. It also can support the growth of hair, skin and nails. Comfrey contains allantoin. Allantoin cleanses wounds by removing the destroyed tissue and stimulating tissue repair.

Meaning

The comfrey remedy brings forward a recognition of our beliefs and relationship to authority. Comfrey helps us shift through insight, subconscious patterns and beliefs, and accelerate to meet with new awareness, learning and consciousness. The earth element of comfrey brings to the surface what is hidden and aids us in integrating changes. When working with comfrey as a remedy I am reminded of an adult that is responsible without being burdened. Comfrey supports clear, defined boundaries of roles within relationships. It helps bring awareness to judgement by perceiving how we judge and are impacted by judgement.

Cress
Cardamine hirsuta

Essence

Bright, sharp, awakens the mind, seeing a way through to right action. Enables the ability to be disciplined without being overbearing or harsh on yourself or others.

Use

Helps to clear the mind after long hours on the computer or being in business meetings. Use when the mind is sluggish or when you feel tired and are having trouble resting. It helps you to rest and to transition from one activity to another. Helpful for over-tired children and good for recovering from jet lag.

Description

Bittercress is a great little salad weed, its botanical name, *cardamine*, is from the Greek words for heart and subdue, the plant having once been used as a heart sedative. It is a small rosette-based annual, up to twenty-five centimetres tall, and a member of the mustard family. When in the early spring it flowers, the stems grow upright with few leaves and put forth small white flowers that quickly turn to seed.

Meaning

Bittercress has an alert, fluid quality. It is responsive and connects us to our hearts. It reminds us that our actions are best when we are aligned with our hearts. The nature of bitter cress is bright, sharp, of the trickster, and playful.

Bittercress helps us to take action at the right time while also allowing space to be restful. The remedy helps us to examine how we act and what we are acting from. It gives us clarity and perception, shows up rigidity and holds us to account. Bittercress creates a pathway towards the notion of embodiment. It has the ability to go through immense change and yet stays true to the essence.

Dandelion
Taraxacum officinale

Essence

Enables you to feel grounded and relaxed so you are able to respond appropriately to your surroundings.

Use

Use for shock, particularly when there has been a sudden change in circumstance. It is excellent to use when thoughts and actions are scattered. Dandelion can bring back focus and re-establish inner peace. It helps children and adults recover from shyness, particularly in big crowds or when there is a feeling of overwhelm in social situations. It clarifies personal boundaries and helps discern collective and personal emotions when participating in group process.

Description

Dandelion possesses a hollow stem that supports a brightly emanating composite flower head that is sensitive to the sun, opening at dawn and closing at dusk. Dandelion pertains to the earth. It makes fast to the earth in an upright manner. The stem will grow higher if it is growing amongst tall plants so that when it flowers it may be in the sun. Even the seeds, that are designed to be carried by the wind, have a perfect anchored parachute shape allowing them to float down to earth in an upright manner. The seed head is like a convex station for silvery stars with an earth centre of brown seeds.

The leaves are without hairs and the margins of the leaves are jagged like teeth where one of its folk names, 'lion's teeth', come from. The leaves grow close to the ground in a floret. Dandelion has a long history as a healing plant. Its botanical name, *taraxacum*, is derived from Greek *taraxos* meaning disorder and *akos*, remedy.

Meaning

Dandelion's essence is nourishment. It contains the qualities of both the earth and the sun. The dandelion remedy enables relaxation throughout the body, knowing all is well. It is a tonic that allows us to access joy within the body. It reminds us to celebrate with others and to stretch out when despondent.

On the physical plane, dandelion helps clear toxins from the body. On the energetic plane, it helps us to shift the energetic toxins and challenges of the modern world. Its strength is that it stays fully connected to all aspects of itself and therefore helps integration after a spiritual process, healing or states of shock.

Scotch thistle
Cirsium vulgare

Essence

This is a remedy for relationship. It evokes actions aligned to the heart. There is a clarity in when to protect, and an experience of joyousness.

Use

Scotch thistle can be used in handling difficult work relationships. It helps with being able to communicate and hold your own with bullies, over-bearing bosses, people who impinge on personal space. Gives insight and clarity when faced with confusion and obfuscation. Use for children when they are dealing with bullies and where they are needing to find their own individual sense of self. Aids recovery from depression.

Description

In New Zealand, this is one of our most abundant thistles. It is a biennial, germinating in early spring. In its first summer it forms a rosette. In its second summer, between November and March, it flowers. The composite flower heads are purple and the seeds are attached to feathery down that is carried by the wind. The leaves of the scotch thistle are spiny on the upper surface. It has deep lobes, tipped with strong spines. It has a strong central taproot. Scotch thistle can grow quite large, forming well-branched shrubs up to a metre and a half high.

Meaning

The essence of scotch thistle contains feelings of joyousness and invincibility. When I observe the whole plant, there is an uprightness and aliveness that makes you want to celebrate, even if life is full of challenges. It seems to say, 'yes I am alive and I have cause to celebrate'. It helps raise your energy – particularly when you have that feeling of being sunk down to the pit of your stomach. The scotch thistle remedy offers courage for those who have suffered and survived hardship, bringing feelings of hope and life force. It contains a quality of elation yet has a feisty edge. It aids us to let go of all the non-essentials and just step forward.

Native Plants

The plants in this series of remedies are all made from the coastal broadleaf forest on Waiheke Island. Forests of Aotearoa, New Zealand, are unique in that 80% of the c 2300 species of flora are found nowhere else in the world. Most of the flowers of these plants are small, greenish to white, and attract moths and flies. Some, like the kōtukutuku, are pollinated by tūī and bellbirds. The fruits, however, tend to be colourful and fleshy to attract birds. I like to remember that our forests evolved with birds and moths rather than mammals. Forests are a collective and in making these essences I am always aware of the quality of the plant's essence in relationship to its place within a wider community of trees, shrubs, ferns and palms.

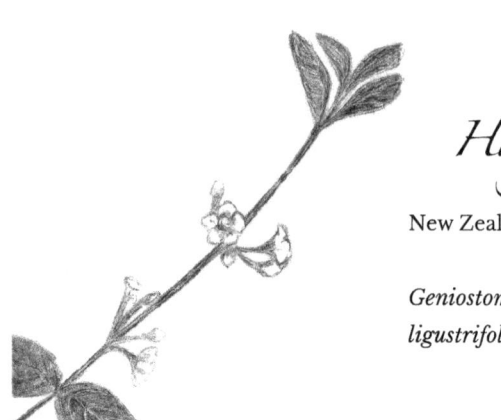

Hangehange

New Zealand Privet

Geniostoma rupestre var. ligustrifolium

Essence

There is a timeless quality to hangehange. It allows a space to open, a reflection to occur as we transition from place to place or activity to activity. It invites us to slow down and arrive into a different pace.

Use

Hangehange is particularly good for children who go at a different pace to those around them. It is also useful for parents to adjust to a slower pace and give space and time with their children. It is helpful when we feel overloaded. I find it supports learning processes, particularly the challenges of learning new things. It helps us to receive, integrate and extend our abilities around information.

Description

Hangehange is a small tree with shining pale green leaves and slender brittle branches. It grows up to 4m in height and is classified as a bushy shrub as it tends to have a thin trunk. In a dry summer, the leaves wilt and yet it seems to survive a drought well. I love the softness of its appearance and the green of its leaves, which are light under the canopy of a coastal forest.

The leaves are opposite, pointed and oval. The scent of its greenish-white flowers is sweet in the spring. The fruit develop in summer. They are black capsules, which split into two valves. When the seed capsule opens, it reveals only the dark seed tips held within an enlarged pulpy placenta.

Meaning

Trust in the space before words. Trust in the unknown. Hangehange allows a sensitivity to the presence of something different, an otherworldliness, a valve if you like between the dimensions, and it can swing open. This remedy leads you to self-acceptance, and a greater ability to accept others without the need to project or use your will to change them. Hangehange illuminates where there is illusion, showing up convoluted pathways and unnecessary complications.

Karamu
Coprosma robusta

Essence

The karamu remedy helps us access our creative source and supports the expression of our creativity. It enables one to realize what is nourishing, to become present and act in alignment.

Use

For when we cannot move forward due to obstacles. An excellent remedy for those who are unable to do simple actions, and for those who become fixated on the obstacles rather than being able to start doing the actions needed in realizing their life.

Description

Karamū is in the Coprosma family (the coffee family). Settlers used the berries to make coffee. The fruit is sweet, with the seed giving a slightly bitter aftertaste. Karamū is widely distributed throughout New Zealand, its fruit is a valuable food source for birds, and it prefers the forest margins, as it won't thrive in the shade. Bellbirds, tūī, silvereyes, blackbirds and thrushes disperse the seed.

Meaning

Tough, rough and resilient, it enables us to keep growing through difficult circumstances. It is a sun-loving plant, lifting depression. Karamū is helpful when the mind is obsessing on detail. It has an expansive quality, allowing us to experience space when we may feel closed in or trapped. Its essence is confirming and helps you to stay on track.

I notice that it can help perceive the wound in our heart and aid, through our presence, to begin to clean the wound and shift stagnant and old emotions. It can aid your posture. Use for those who are sunken over the chest area, shoulders hunched, or those who too often hold their breath.

Kōtukutuku

New Zealand Tree Fuchsia
Fuchsia excorticata

Essence

Connection through gratitude. Harmony through understanding our separation. Valuing our own and each other's contribution towards the whole of a project or building of culture.

Use

Kōtukutuku is beneficial when we experience that we are not being valued and when we forget to value another.

Description

Excorticata is Latin for peeling bark. The bark is light coloured, sometimes almost red in colour, and is fibrous and stringy. The flower of kōtukutuku is beautiful; it has a combination of magenta hues to mauve, blues and violet. Its pollen is an intense pure blue; the flowers are pollinated by the tūī and bellbird. It is one of the few deciduous trees in New Zealand. It grows from sea level up to about 1,000 m, particularly alongside creeks and rivers. Kōtukutuku are easily recognized by the characteristic appearance of their bark, which peels spontaneously, hanging in red papery strips to show a pale wood underneath. The edible fruit in Māori is kōnini, and the name is sometimes given to the tree as well. European settlers used the berries to make jam and puddings.

Meaning

Kōtukutuku embodies grace and mana. It allows tension to drop, particularly where there is constriction of the self within relationships. There is a discovery of one's mana, an inner confidence. Through playfulness, you can free yourself from the social strictures that have been put on you. It aids in handling and being present to grief, particularly where loss causes us to discard ourselves.

A threshold is the strip of wood or stone forming the bottom of a doorway and crossed when entering a house or room. Sometimes in nature we experience such a threshold as if we are crossing from one room to another. I notice when taking kōtukutuku I become more attuned when crossing these subtle thresholds; it brings insight into the different qualities of energy in places.

This kotukutuku remedy brings awareness to where our ego has become unbalanced and has become detrimental to our relationships. It enables discipline to occur in a natural way. Kōtukutuku helps us to recognize and respect each aspect that contributes to our life. This respect reflects back to us in the form of beauty and grace in our life.

Nīkau
Rhopalostylis sapida

Essence

Nīkau brings a natural reverence for the ordinary aspects of life. It creates a nourishing structure with beauty of design to help you flourish in your life. Nīkau brings forward the knowledge of community, that we need interdependent relationships and non-exclusive processes to build healthy groups and community.

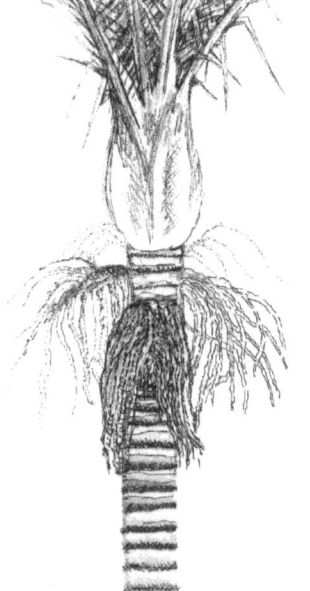

Use

Use for experiences of separation and isolation, or when we feel disconnected from our purpose. Nīkau allows us to see the purpose of boundaries. At the same time, it opens us to the realization that everything is interconnected.

Description

Nīkau is New Zealand's only species of native palm. It's also the world's most southern naturally-growing palm. The leaves are fronds, and the trunk is ringed by the frond scars. The flowers bloom in the early spring and are enclosed in two spathes. The flowers are arranged in groups of three along the inflorescent branches. Each group comprises a small female flower sitting in-between two male flowers. The male flowers drop off and the female flowers open later. When it fruits, the kererū love the small red berries.

Meaning

Nīkau aids in an acceptance of difference, which has the effect of both softening and defining the boundaries. Boundaries become natural rather than imposed. Through acceptance of difference, an innate respect arises. Nīkau is resilient and deeply rooted. It represents the quality of staying in one place and the contribution to the place and community that comes from being settled. Knowledge can be gained by spending time in one place. Nīkau brings an understanding that everything is in relationship to everything else, that we can't change reality to our liking. This is a remedy that is helpful for those who demand that the world bend to their will. It wakes them up to see that they can't push the river against its flow and that there is abundance and nourishment in the proper way. It encourages a more community-anchored action grounded in a wider vision of consequence.

Pōhuehue
Muehlenbeckia complexa

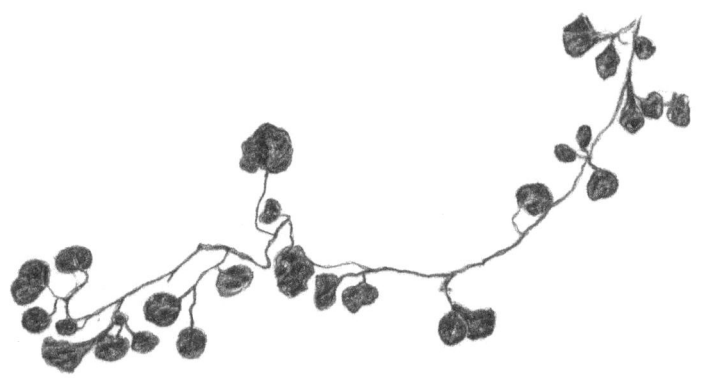

Essence

Pōhuehue allows for a forward movement with deep purpose. This is realized through a playful response to life with a natural weave of mind and heart.

Use

This remedy is particularly helpful for clarifying a course of action when we feel confused. It is helpful when we become too caught up in our mind, are assumptive, overly critical or even paranoid. Pōhuehue invites us to become lighter in our outlook and open in our thinking.

Description

Pōhuehue plants form tangled climbing bushes that grow near the sea. It comes from the buckwheat family, a widely distributed family of plants. The leaves and stems are usually acrid or astringent. The stems are climbing, divaricating, interlacing and slender. The heart-shaped leaves are one to two centimetres long. The flowers are cream coloured and dioecious, forming into succulent white translucent fruit surrounding a black seed.

Meaning

Sometimes a remedy takes you by surprise and pōhuehue can be like this, for it acts upon our intuition. This remedy helps us to identify the overriding patterns and perceptions that we live by. It brings awareness to the assumptions we make about others or events. The ability to see our own negative thinking gives us the ability to change. This, in turn, leads to an exuberant response to life and an intensifying of perceptions. Pōhuehue also creates empathy, enabling you to get inside an object and experience it. The expansion that pōhuehue brings is through a sense of protection and safety, a sense of being connected to a good place within ourselves.

Ponga
Cyathea dealbata

Essence

This remedy opens the doorway into the mystical dimensions through being fully present in the physical world. It enables a free-ranging meditative state of mind through an anchored stillness.

Use

An excellent remedy for those drawn into other people's worlds and those who lose their own sense of self. Ponga enhances our state of being and experience. Careful use of this remedy is recommended. It is particularly useful for working with depression. It works to enhance other remedies. Use for when we lose trust in our lives.

Description

The ponga is a tree fern and is often the first plant to cover land that has been burnt for pasture. The trunk is known as a caudex, and it can grow up to 9 to 10 metres tall. The caudex is very fibrous and the upper portion has the bases of old frond stems, called stipes. Ponga are robust, often re-growing after being cut down. The fronds are erect; the sori large, brown and covered by a dome-like indusium. Mature ponga form buttresses at the base with a dense mass of aerial roots.

Meaning

The ponga remedy is about an earth-based spiritual exploration. As the ponga frond unfurls, it is a koru, a spiral form that contains its innate power that can only be expressed. It does not interrupt itself. Fluid and unstoppable, it reflects the nature and power to live and to exist without argument or denial. As this unfolds, it's transformative. There's forward movement and all we have to do is be still and allow it. How to be in it, is to be centred in ourselves and trusting of the life force that propels us forward.

This remedy is balanced, but more than that, it centres us into the life force. Ponga also creates the nursery for further life. It is, therefore, a great remedy for getting projects moving and being able to focus your attention on what is most important for the project to move forward. The balance shows in the gesture, the strength and solidness of the caudex and the lightness of the fronds.

Insects

Insects are the most diverse group of animals, including more than a million described species and represent over half of all known living organisms. Yet few people take the time to get to know them and many consider them pests. In bringing forward this range of remedies, I aim to examine our relationship with these insects, and hope to change our view a little. It's worthwhile to connect and observe their gesture, their habits, and in doing so, see their participation and contribution to the world we inhabit. All of these remedies are created energetically through the conduit of water and are then preserved in brandy. They have been made with the living insect nearby; each remedy has the energetic vibration of the insect, and each has its own unique story.

Bee
Apis mellifera

Essence

Knowing your expertise within a social context. Balancing individuality and self-determination with working towards the common good of a community or enterprise.

Use

Use for when there is a conflict of ideas that block progress in a project or enterprise. Bee works to help identify the shadow-self at work within a relationship and helps to transform that by recognizing the part that we play in the outcome of our lives and relationships.

Description

A whole hive hums and resonates, and you can have hives next to each other, and yet a bee knows which hive they belong to.
The bee has antennae with powerful sense organs for touch and smell. Recent research has found that they possess a plastic sense of smell – that they can discern shapes through scent. Bees are sensitive to electrical fields and can sense the earth's magnetic fields, which they use in navigation and possibly comb building.

The worker bees carry their own weight in nectar and pollen. Each worker visits approximately a thousand flowers every day. The duties of the workers are multitudinous. They are the builders, brood nurses, honey makers, pollen stampers, guards, porters and foragers.

Meaning

The bee is an individual acting for the whole. When we bring that wisdom to ourselves we begin to understand that we are not separate, even though we see ourselves as individual. There is a strong sense that the bee knows where they belong, they know their work and their role. The bee remedy supports us in accessing our own life force. It shows us how one small part is connected to the whole, one aspect of pattern within a bigger pattern, a vibrating interconnection to a vast detailed ecosystem. It enables us to experience our environment through movement and the life force all around.

Bees call attention to what is important and to attend to what has been neglected. There is an experience of abundance in this remedy in that it offers a connection to source and an understanding of unity. It allows a knowledge of receptivity and nourishment through an encounter with a rich, mellifluous life force. This remedy expresses a sense of joy and peacefulness, supporting a pathway of action that we may have been blind to.

Cicada

Kihikihi wawā
Amphipsalta zealandica

Essence

Allows for the individual to experience the space of the inner being, being the instrument rather than the player.

Use

When we let resistance take power in our lives, take the cicada remedy to enable you to surrender into and be able to do the projects and actions that are close to your soul's purpose despite the resistance. Cicada pulls us into equilibrium and is useful when, like Icarus, we fly too close to the sun.

Description

This remedy was made in the midst of the deafening roar of the cicada. It was a remarkable soundscape amongst the dry kanuka. It is the male cicadas that sing whilst the females will answer the male with wing clicks. Each male has its own distinctive song so that the species can locate the correct mates. In *New Zealand Insects and Their Story,* Richard Sharell describes how the sound is created: "On the underside of the abdomen there are two half-rounded scales. These are the lids covering the sound apparatus. Most of the abdomen is hollow, creating a sound box. There is a ridged membrane called a tympanum, and in the upper part, two tightly stretched membranes. Clusters of powerful muscles alternately tighten and release the tension on these membranes, causing a vibration, which is amplified by the air chamber."

The life cycle of the cicada begins with the female depositing her eggs into the bark by creating a cavity with her sharp ovipositor. When the tiny larvae hatch, they fall to the ground and burrow into the soil until they find a root to attach to and suck the sap. Three to seven years is spent in total darkness, feeding, moulting and growing. In the final moult, the wing pads are formed. With its powerful forelegs, it then digs its way to the surface, climbs up a stem and anchors to the support. Usually during the night, the skin splits at the back and the adult emerges.

Meaning

This remedy brings us to experience surrender, the art of surrender. It celebrates the completion of a cycle. Letting go of the difficulty, the bitterness of hard times and allowing warmth and happiness to seep in. Intuition is enhanced with a greater awareness of messages received. It will work with the senses that you are dominant in. If you are a visionary, you will get clearer visionary messages.

Cricket

Pihareinga
Teliogryllus commodus

Essence

Courage to act, moving forwards to adventure and exploration; releasing self- restriction, particularly where we have created our own rules and constraints from our past; being able to work with the past and past events, releasing what holds us and finding the good and useful from this.

Use

Cricket remedy works well when taken over the space of a few days, particularly when experiencing being stuck and unable to act. It is helpful for anxiety – particularly in a social context where old patterns of socialization and old relationships may be encountered. Cricket also attends to the soul when there has been soul loss due to ostracization and where, through past experiences of inadequacy and aloneness in groups, there is an inability to feel supported in community. Cricket gives the courage to be present and participate in community and groups.

Cricket is helpful in the face of chaos and when your actions become futile. Use in busy workplaces where you find yourself jumping to other people's stress and urgency. Try cricket at work and see how you get on.

Description

Crickets comes from the order of Orthoptera, which means straight wings. Crickets have big thighed, jumping hind legs, and ears in the shins of the forelegs. The chorus of sound heard is created by the rasping structures at the base of the male's forewings, which are rapidly drawn over each other creating friction, while the wings are held up at an angle. During the day, crickets shelter in cracked ground or under convenient objects.

The female deposits her eggs in the cracked ground during late summer and autumn. There they overwinter, hatching in October and feeding on ground vegetation. Their wings develop gradually until they mature in mid-summer. Crickets grow by shedding their skin on a regular basis. After each moult the crickets utilize the trace elements contained in the skin by eating it.

Meaning

This remedy can reveal unconscious material and point towards the shadow in an issue. It gives the ability to work with the past, to see the past events and incidences that are hard to integrate and fully move through. It helps us forward by allowing us to see the good and the useful in our situation. Cricket shines a light in the darkness. It helps in times when we feel blind and can only go from one point to another without seeing the bigger picture. It gives the ability to take in what life presents to us and transmute it.

Praying Mantis

Miomantis caffra

Essence

Awakening to tricks and patterns of our thinking, extended awareness through observation and an inner stillness.

Use

Use when past choices are impacting your ability to move forward; when there are persistent negative thought patterns; emerging from addiction, particularly alcohol; and emerging from relationships that have become toxic or sour. This remedy will help you find your stillness and support you to be alone, giving space for aspects of your inner to emerge.

Description

There are two species of praying mantis found in New Zealand. The native praying mantis, which has a blue patch on the inside of its front legs, and the South African praying mantis, introduced from South Africa in 1978. The native adults don't survive the winter, whereas the African one does, giving it an advantage.

The mantis is unusual in the insect world in that it can turn its head in all directions, examining and inspecting. It has two large compound eyes, while on the vertex of the head, three simple eyes, ocelli, form a small triangle.

During the late summer, the abdomen of the female swells with ripening eggs. In creating its egg case the mantis sits perfectly still, and almost imperceptibly lifts the tip of the abdomen and exudes a whitish-brown foamy substance. The egg case is brown at the sides and the egg chambers, arranged two abreast, are covered with a whitish lid. About twenty to twenty-five eggs are sealed in the chambers. In the late autumn, the female dies. In the spring, the larvae hatch into minute images of the adults, lacking only the wings.

Meaning

This remedy was made after spending time observing a pregnant female praying mantis. I was mesmerized by her swaying focus, movement and stillness, perfectly at play. She seemed to be undisturbed by my presence, and time felt adrift. I was coming into her presence rather than her into mine. I had the uncanny experience of feeling myself observed by her. For a moment I wanted to go away. The *I am so busy* mantra started playing in my head. There is something about being caught by the gaze of the praying mantis that is disarming, and it was this that made me sit deeply in her presence and then ask permission that I may work with her essence.

Praying mantis integrates our ability to perceive the existence of a creative energy of the universe as part of the physical world. It brings reflection into the fulcrum, the point of balance that can happen in a day, perhaps in a year, a timing within our life, of stillness, and an opening to choose.

Chinese Paper Wasp
Polistes chinensis

Essence

The aesthetics of attending to the physical form. This remedy assists in maintaining personal boundaries.

Use

The paper wasp remedy is particularly helpful for those who absorb other people's emotions and energies. This is an excellent remedy when you are unwell and needing to take space to heal.

Description

The Chinese paper wasp is black with vivid yellow stripes. It has a very thin tapered waist and its wings droop down. It builds its nests above ground, which are made up of paper-like octagon-shaped cells. This remedy was made in the early summer from a busy family of female wasps feeding their larvae in a growing colony in the eaves of a friend's house. The wasps hovered and crawled around the rim of the small glass that I was using.

Wasp colonies tend to die out during winter, restarting each spring. During the winter, the young males and females hibernate, clinging to the underside of the abandoned nest. In the spring, the females, whether fertilized or not, help construct the new nest and the males die. The fertilized queens deposit eggs into the new cells and then assist the unfertilized workers, gathering honeydew to feed to the larvae. As the larvae develop, the adults feed them macerated, protein-rich food like cicadas and caterpillars. When fully grown, the larvae spin a silken cover over the entrance of the cell and pupate. The adults that emerge are all females. At the end of the season, the queen lays unfertilized eggs, which turn into males.

Meaning

When I take the wasp remedy and sit with it, my first experience is a sense of my own consciousness looking out from my body. I am in my body and acutely aware of my surroundings. I become aware of texture, qualities of softness and hardness, I see relationships through their physical existence. I see the natural order in how each object touches another. As I become aware of this, I experience a settling. I become aware of my bones. It's like my bones settle themselves as if they are saying *oh finally you have decided to be at home today*. The etheric quality of the physical becomes available to observe and be with. This essence invites us to reflect on our mistakes, taking responsibility for ourselves, transforming weaknesses into strengths. Wasp looks after itself first. It initiates, with a powerful reminder that the sting can push us into action that is better aligned to ourselves.

Tree Wētā

Pūtangatanga
Hemideina thoracica

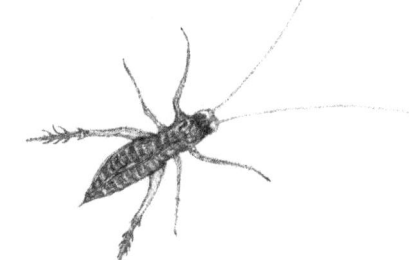

Essence

Tree wētā enables acute awareness of where there is disturbance in the natural balance of relationships; to perceive where our actions and understandings are influenced by another, and observe shifts and balances of power within relationships.

Use

Relationships over time form their own patterns. Often we can't see these patterns because we become used to behaviours and how we respond and react to them. Use wētā remedy when you feel stuck in a relationship, and for loosening out of a co-dependent relationship. This remedy helps us to see how to be present with change, and how to see through patterns of fear and deception. Use for when we are seeking and looking beyond what we already have. It allows us to access the capacity within us for change.

Description

The tree wētā is the streetwise wētā, it lives in gardens and in the bush. Its life revolves around its shelter holes in hollow trees and hollow stems. It tends to hide during the day and night, feeding on succulent bark, foliage and occasionally other insects. Some possess tunnels, occupied by a single wētā, usually a male that welcomes females and occasionally juveniles but defends it against rival males.

The females probe the soil and lay their eggs usually in the autumn after the rain, when the soil is not hard and dry. The eggs hatch into baby wētā, who do a series of moults over the next 12–18 months. The juveniles look like tiny versions of the adults.

Tree wētā create sound by raising and lowering the hind legs so that a rasping structure on the inner surface of the femurs passes over a corresponding area of the sides of the abdomen. It is quite something in the evening to realize that the unusual clicking sound you are hearing is, in fact, a wētā.

Meaning

The wētā remedy enables fluidity where we have become frozen. It warms and moves what has been frozen through trauma, allowing a coming back into life. The feeling in taking this essence is a connection to an ancient source; to see things from this perspective allows us to understand the transient nature of life. It supports the ability to go deeper into issues without losing the overall vision. It helps in perceiving the role we take in relationships and realizing we have choice in being able to shift out of these roles. This remedy may bring up shadows that lie hidden, to face the truth, even if it's ugly, to move and shift what has been held through hatred and fear. It can be very powerful, and I recommend that you take time to be aware of your reactions to others and nourish yourself, particularly if some deep emotional memories come up for you.

To see a World in a Grain of Sand

And a Heaven in a Wild Flower,

Hold Infinity in the Palm of your Hand

And Eternity in an Hour.

William Blake from *Auguries of Innocence* 1803

Minerals

In this collection, land is integral to each essence. A mineral essence contains a story; sometimes it's mythic, it weaves place and time, it accesses the universe, it reminds us of the microcosm within the macrocosm, the above as is below, like the lines of Blake's poetry.

Minerals are integral to the material world and society. They give us stability, structure and balance. They can also create rifts in our relationships, feelings of superiority and unhappiness. Awareness and understanding of our relationship with the material world can lead to cooperation without the need to renounce or discard. I often think that what balances all that power and strength of the material force is tenderness.

Rock is universal. It is the stuff of the universe, a fundamental element of life, star dust. Merging with a mineral or rock through meditation is to experience a great dropping away of what we identify with in the world. Paradoxically, the mineral and the material world is what we create from to express our identity. None of these remedies can be remade, for time, season, land and story are innately woven into each of them.

Chambered Nautilus
Nautilus pompilius

Essence

An experience of connection to a divine force that flows into ordinary life, bringing insight and synchronicity.

Use

For times when external events disrupt our ability to find our way. Chambered nautilus opens us up to a structure that allows stillness within and from this place to act aligned to a purpose. It builds back self-love and respect after experiences that have led to shame and desolation. Use for displacement, loss of home and when one's place has been taken or destroyed. This remedy also helps people who have been made to feel guilty through projection and blame.

Description

Nautili are considered to be living fossils. They first appeared about 500 million years ago during the Cambrian epoch. The graceful shell, from which this essence is made, is a nearly perfect equiangular spiral or logarithmic spiral. The curvature follows this logarithmic spiral with each turn being exactly three times the size of the one below it. The size of the spiral increases, but its shape is unaltered with each successive curve.

Nautili start creating their shell as soon as they hatch. It begins about the size of a pea, and at each successive stage of its development, the nautilus moves into a new chamber and seals off the old chamber. These chambers are gas-filled flotation chambers and each is connected by a small tube, which acts like a siphon, regulating the density of gas, enabling the nautilus to control its buoyancy.

It moves shell first, so it can't see where it is going. The nautilus spends the day hiding down in the depths of the ocean, approximately 400 metres down. At night they ascend to the surface to feed. They have tentacles that can smell and manipulate and they also have highly developed chemical senses that can detect predators and food. Octopuses are their main predator. Nautili are rare and protected.

Meaning

The key to this remedy is the spiral structure of the nautilus. It is through this that we may reach for support as we find ourselves stuck in negative grooves and patterns that seem at a variance to our purpose. This remedy helps us access the totality and sudden flashes of inspiration that can shift us swiftly from one state to another. The spiral is a symbol of life always in movement. The spiral is at the beginning of our life. We emerge from water, as the first substance, and the vortical energy of matter and consciousness, and also disappear into it at the end. Within us is the continuum of the consciousness of the beginning and the whole.

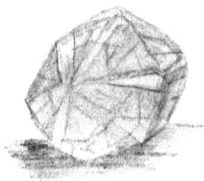 

Essence

The transient nature of life; light and beauty; the celebration of beauty through our participation in the world rather than the desire to own or capture it.

Use

Use for clearing spaces, particularly when experiencing heavy or suppressing energy. Diamond brings to light the desire for power-over or where there has been a misuse of power. It is helpful when discerning a ghost that has attached to a place or person due to resonance.

Description

This remedy was created at Te Waikoropupū Springs near Tākaka. As I walked through Te Waikoropupū Reserve, carrying the essence through the forest, the soft rain was falling and the sun was slanting through the rain. The small droplets of water on the leaves with the sun shining through created shimmering, sparkling diamonds in every drop of water. Those droplets of rain that hung from the leaves of the forest plants touched the clear glass and ran into the glass bowl, mixing with the diamond and the water I'd collected from a small outlet of the springs. Natural diamonds, such as the one used in this remedy, are formed at high temperature at depths of 140–190km in the earth's mantle. They are brought close to the earth's surface through volcanic activity.

Meaning

Reverence, tenderness and respect are the feelings we have when we are met and meet a sacred place or when we create a sacred relationship. To desecrate is to treat a place or person with violent disrespect. Diamond is hard and sharp. There is no closing one's eyes from the pain of desecration. Diamond helps us to name it and redress it.

The essence of diamond, through intention, can begin to clear where there has been genocide or where there has been a misuse of power through the ancestral line. This remedy taken during and after work on ancestral lineage will support and integrate the shifts that occur through insight and revelation. It can enable us the strength and courage to acknowledge difficult issues pertaining to colonisation and misuse of power. It can be used when you are a victim of theft, either physically or psychically.

The diamond works deep within the inner qualities of the spirit. Diamond can be a source of inspiration, while at the same time uncovering our fragility. For me, it opens up a tenderness where I sense the fragmented, tattered wings of my soul through the light of the inner that stretches like the milky way across a clear night.

Pearl

Essence

Pearl affects who we are through understanding that we are a relationship between events and things. The way we perceive is through a rich spectrum of our interactions with others, memory and ancestral memory. Pearl gifts us a fluid consciousness.

Use

Pearl helps us see our mistakes and supports reflection and integration around them. The mistake, therefore, becomes revelatory and enables change to happen. It helps us to stand true to ourselves in the face of deception or obfuscation. Use pearl to create a sacred space for personal rituals and spiritual practice. It may be used to help clear, energetically, places that have been desecrated.

Description

This remedy was made above Mawhitipana Bay on Waiheke Island. Using saltwater I placed it on the headland between the two beaches facing north. It was an evening of the full moon and was made as the sun was setting and the moon was rising so that at one point both were there at the edge of the horizon. I used three pearls.

A pearl is made up of calcium carbonate and is deposited within soft tissue in concentric circles – the pearl forms as a defence mechanism against an irritant like a parasite inside its shell. The mollusc creates the pearl to seal off the irritant.

Meaning

The shadow of this remedy is deception, and in taking this remedy we may begin to peel away the dross, perceiving what is underneath and the intention behind actions. Pearl opens pathways of memory and ancestral knowledge within ourselves. It enables us to uphold our intuitive capability and listen to inner promptings. It helps us to protect creative processes, trusting the right timing to emerge. It opens up our perception of time to an eternal experience of time. This allows space to communicate and also connect with our essential nature.

Pounamu

Essence

The essence of pounamu is the heart. It is about accessing unconditional love through our vulnerability. The need to protect is gently shifted to an alignment. This alignment is like a settling, pieces being put into their place.

Use

In times of conflict, pounamu allows us to remember that harmonious relationships did exist. It supports assimilation of challenging and difficult circumstances. It supports people to act with integrity and incorruptibility. It assists those who struggle to access their intrinsic self. When people cannot access that inner quality, they become reliant on others to boost their self-esteem. They will sometimes merge with another, or mimic. The pounamu remedy leads them back within themselves.

Description

Pounamu is found only in the South Island of New Zealand. There lies īnanga pounamu – pearly white, translucent, the little freshwater fish *Galaxias maculatus*; kahurangi pounamu – a vivid shade of green, the clearness of sky; kawakawa pounamu

– the leaves of kawakawa with all the shades, the flecks and inclusions; and tangiwai pounamu – clear glass tears that come from great sorrow. Geologically, the two main types of pounamu are nephrite and bowenite. The pounamu-bearing rocks were raised to the earth's surface by movement and collision along a plate boundary and the rock was eroded through the action of streams, rivers and past glaciers. As with all the mineral essences, it incorporates the land where it was made. This remedy was made from a kawakawa pounamu under a pōhutukawa tree above Pūtiki Bay on Waiheke Island.

Meaning

Feelings of self-consciousness, and sensitivity to how others may be perceiving us, are put into perspective. The pounamu remedy pertains to the existence of beauty even when we cannot see it. Pounamu brings forward empathy. It integrates the elements of water and mineral. Water has the attributes of immersion. Through the element of water we immerse ourselves in an experience. The positive qualities of this are that we can stay connected to what we know as ourselves and be able to discern what we are merging with. This merging 'with' helps us to understand the quality of the other as separate yet connected to ourselves. This enables us to be more fluid in our ability to not only merge with something but to also let it go. There is courage to walk in peace, to find truth, and to communicate uncomfortable insights that transform communities, enabling a wholistic perception.

greywacke

Essence

Timeless observation. Visionary and grounded. It's a remedy of the east, fostering breakthroughs in understanding and enabling a movement forward.

Use

Use pyramid rock for indecision, when fear and anxiety arise around choices and for inner conflict. This essence enables people to have the courage to create, it brings the visionary capacity forward so that you are able to vision how to act. Use for when perfectionism blocks the ability to act. Gives protection from negative influence.

Description

The pyramid rock is named simply because it is in the shape of a pyramid. It was found at Enclosure Bay, Waiheke Island and is greywacke sandstone. I started the process of creating this remedy at 5.00 a.m. on 28th July 2002. The tide was coming in and I placed the rock on a small rocky tidal island. It was a clear pre-dawn, Matariki (Pleiades) sparkling in the east. In being present with the making of this remedy I had a vision of a feminine presence. She imbued everything with a quality of compassionate love. The remedy stayed on the small tidal island for three and a half hours while the tide came in. The ocean, the stars and the early morning light were vital elements to this remedy.

Meaning

This remedy opens the capacity to vision whilst experiencing a grounded balanced state of being. In taking this remedy there is a connection to time, it seems time is eternal. As I settle into the experience of the remedy, I sense the constant rhythms and patterns that are forever changing as all things physical; evolve, breakdown shift and pass through the elements. They may settle into earth or mingle with air. There is a natural contemplative inner state that slowly emerges revealing new perspectives and therefore allows the mind to let go the past and be present. I love the sense this remedy has of being anchored. When the heart and the visionary mind are connected our insights and ideas have a sense of being able to land and are meaningful. It strengthens your inner purpose through understanding. Pyramid Rock remedy enhances inner observation of our emotions and thoughts. It can enable us to sit with our inner conflicts realising what is at work underneath these experiences. It brings awareness of the patterns and structures that are outmoded and hinder us in our lives.

Rose Quartz

Essence

Rose quartz enables us to move into an uncomfortable place, where through reflection, we can perveive our shadow and how it plays out in our lives. Acknowledging unconditional love to break through patterns of protection and behaviour that constrict us.

Use

This remedy has the ability to wake us up, particularly when we are held in the sway of illusion. Take this essence for boredom. Use for clearing emotional and mental imprinting on land and buildings.

Description

Rose quartz is a mineral composed primarily of silicon dioxide molecules that typically form at about 400–700 degrees Celsius. It forms as magma cools and the silicon dioxide crystallizes. Slow cooling allows the crystals to grow larger. This type of quartz can vary from a pale pink to a rose red hue. The colour is usually due to trace elements of titanium, iron or manganese.

Meaning

It was through clearing the energy from a home and the surrounding land when I perceived the impact of negative internal loops of mind upon the physical object. The home and the land had become a reflection of an inner turmoil of worry and distraction. Rose quartz reflects back how thoughts can penetrate and disturb landscape. Like an unassuming presence, it shows up the misalignment, the skipping over the heart. Rose quartz reveals the imbalance that emerges when we extend our shadow into life and our physical surrounds. The shadow can be like the will, pre-empting events, working away without trust or real connection. These mistakes go against our inner listening and cause disharmony in both the outer and inner worlds. Rose quartz can soften the edges, enabling movement between two opposing points of view. It allows honesty when reflecting on a relationship. It can help to take a step back from an entangled relationship and review from a distance. This remedy reflects truth through unconditional love.

Birds

Remedy making is a curious process, a way of listening, trusting in the inner voice, and opening up a process that engages the essential intelligence that then comes into a unique physical form. Making the bird remedies was different from all my other remedy-making experiences as I found myself embodying the particular bird I was making the remedy from. I also received specific directions and times in the making of these remedies, as the remedies respond to external factors like the moon cycle, daily rhythms and planetary cycles.

The huia is particularly unique in that it is an extinct bird. This was the first bird remedy I made. I came to understand that something that existed in physical form still exists and can be connected to in the present. The last remedy I made was the pīwakawaka (fantail). So often in my journey with the bird remedies, they show up in unusual and unexpected ways.

Huia

Heteralocha acutirostris
(Presumed extinct since 1907)

Essence

Huia opens us to experience how to love someone or something in the entirety of what is presented now, allowing diversity to flourish.

Use

Use for loss and heartbreak occurring through calamitous events. Huia restores connection to the inner, and enables us to find a way through difficult emotional terrain. Huia can be used for the loss of trust and the distortion that occurs through conditional relationships. It also helps to start to perceive a life without abuse (physical, emotional and mental), to perceive beyond narrow and judgmental beliefs.

Description

The story of the huia's extinction is immeasurably sad. It was considered by Māori to be tapu and was associated with the rangatira, the chiefly people. This association meant that the practice of wearing huia feathers became a sign of mana and was adopted by the European population of New Zealand. As the huia feathers gained in popularity, the incentive to hunt huia, combined with habitat loss through large forest burn-offs, caused a collapse in their populations.

In *The Book of the Huia*, W J Phillipps describes the huia as breathtaking in beauty. "Their general bodily colour is dark blue merging to black, with an iridescent greenish sheen covering the anterior parts and sometimes extending on to the tail. When fully mature, the wattles measure nearly an inch across and are bright orange." The huia was the only bird in the world in which the male and the female had beaks of different types, the female bill being significantly longer and curved.

Meaning

The first time I started to work with this remedy I experienced the female with her curved beak leading her way into my body, down through my left side, clearing something out. In this process I experienced strength and gentleness. I also found myself embodying the male and I felt open and stripped away. The experience left me with the impression that nothing could be hidden. I was entirely seen, all aspects that I had shame about. I had been seen and there was no hiding.

This remedy is about love and how to live in the presence of love, how love grows on one another and how as we grow, the love may emanate outwards. Huia provides powerful support for the role of being a woman and the capacity of understanding and responding to community through being a woman. The remedy pertains to sensual love, care, attendance to physical form, sacred acknowledgement of sexuality, and birth and child-raising. It also aids the creation of a pathway to bring back the love, and the power to women and men who have been shamed, broken or feel contaminated through abuse.

North Island Kākā

Nestor meridionalis septentrionalis

Essence

Dispelling illusion; facing truth; fearless, having no qualms; looking at what is hidden; joyous, intelligent and playful.

Use

For times of confusion, disharmony and to support a breakthrough from self-deception, also where there has been a loss of connection to one's truth within groups and community.

Description

The kākā is a forest parrot. They were abundant in the forested areas of New Zealand but their numbers rapidly declined as forests were burned for pasture and exotic pine plantations, even up until the 1970s. They have only recently returned to Waiheke Island, from Little Barrier Island, as the land is slowly reforesting. They like to gather in groups and are active and social in the early morning and evening. They are partially nocturnal and I hear their call in the night. Kākā are omnivorous. During the day they feed, solitary and silent, using their powerful beaks to tear off loose bark, breaking up decaying wood and extracting larvae from live wood. They also eat many kinds of seeds, succulent fruits and have a brush tongue to take nectar from flowers.

Meaning

Kākā initiates. Kākā invites us to have the courage to look. The truth is often concealed by the stories we live by and the roles we play out in our communities. Its qualities can be sudden and revelatory – particularly in seeing the hidden agreements made around people's stories and where a group can be manipulated through one person's self-deception. This remedy shows up our patterns of avoidance, like a teacher setting us up so we can learn. It brings awareness to boundaries. It shows up the way things are in relation to each other. This quality of perception brings clarity to action through consciousness. Fear of loss is the shadow of kākā – when we lie to ourselves but do not know because we are unconscious. In this darkness there is a distortion, a fear of growth, shadow protection through stories and deception. Kākā can awaken a conscious choice to look at what we may hide from ourselves. Kākā does what it does, straight to what is underneath. If there is sorrow, it is uncovered. If there is fear, it is seen and acknowledged.

Kōtare

New Zealand Kingfisher
Halcyon sancta vagans

Essence

Integrated focus; ability to encompass the whole picture; action arising out of stillness.

Use

Kōtare opens our ability to find stillness, adding a quality of observation of our thinking. This essence is good to take when our life becomes split or when we compartmentalize. It also helps with over-self-analysis, supporting us to find healthy reflective processes. Use for distraction, unproductive busyness, disruption and deflection that causes projects and right-action to falter.

Description

I often see kōtare perched on posts, telephone and power lines, or bare branches. It perches with a clear view, overlooking pasture, gardens and water. They are often still, except their tail will flick, or their head will turn. They are waiting for their prey, usually insects like cicada, mice, also cockabullies and small fish, to appear. Then they are off in a direct descending flight, snatching the prey and carrying it crosswise in their beak back to their perch where they swallow it whole. Kōtare feathers are blue, green and turquoise with a touch of white around the neck and a soft yellow on the breast.

Meaning

The kōtare essence is an ultimate experience in focus, a focus that encompasses the whole. It pertains to our ability to observe with a focus that emerges from our whole participation in our world. To observe without thinking, without the narrative bubbling away. This alert presence is aware of our surroundings, knowing the language of our environment. This remedy invites us to move across rifts, faults and fractures of relationship. It invites us to see and understand compromise and the loss associated with compromise. Kōtare supports our nervous system and can relieve tension and headaches, particularly when triggered by fear. It combines alertness and restfulness, fulfillment experienced through clear action.

Sparrow

Passer domesticus domesticus

Essence

Bringing attention to aspects of ourselves we have neglected; bringing awareness in how we respond to family patterns and collective consciousness; enhances ability to move through difficult situations, keeping connected and integral; encourages agility and inner strength in relationships where there has been a misuse of power or a power imbalance.

Use

For coming out of periods of illness and retreat. The sparrow remedy supports integration into community and social connection. It strengthens the nervous system and helps reduce anxiety due to stress and overload. It opens pathways of communication particularly helpful for shy or reserved people who would like to be heard.

Description

Sparrows were introduced to New Zealand in the mid-1860s, and the house sparrow is now found from sub-arctic to subtropical regions, basically everywhere except western Australia and some islands. Sparrows are a flocking species and are seldom seen alone. Roosting is communal: sometimes numbering several hundred in dense shrubs and trees. The secret to the sparrow's success lies in its close association with people; its nest sites and food supply depend upon human endeavour. It is exceptionally unusual to find sparrows living a long way from human habitation. Male and female sparrows differ in that the male has a conspicuous chestnut streak behind the eye and the upper surface of the wings are predominately brown. The female is a more uniform brown with breast and flanks a soft grey. Sparrows also have one of the closest social structures to people in the animal kingdom. They have long-term loving relationships with who they raise their young. But will have affairs and switch partners.

Meaning

I am a sparrow. I know how to move around. I am impacted by the collective and I am part of the collective, and yet inside of you, I am alone. I am showing you existence. I am showing you aloneness and an awareness of that aloneness. I am also a messenger from your ancestors and can open your awareness to the collective consciousness and your family patterns. I get you reflecting on relationships and marriage and family groupings. I support by bringing you to the details of a project. I remind you of attending to the small, building piece by piece until the greater whole appears. I reach up and peck at your heart. I am the bird that moves into the neglected spaces and brings your awareness to the aspects of your psyche that you have abandoned. I bring awareness to that that has been abandoned, neglected and forgotten. I also work with the physical form and remind you of the relationship between the physical and the metaphysical. I work through the extension of the senses to receive insights into the metaphysical world. I will always find my way out of any place and often find my way in. I do not easily become trapped.

Tui

Prosthemadera novaeseelandiae

Essence

A love and commitment to explore life in its totality; liberating expression; warriorship; clarity of action; face to face fearlessness to those that hold authority; desire and creativity; the joy of communication and expression.

Use

Use when there is a loss of *duende*, an essential quality of life force; when feeling defeated and over-ridden by another; when there is an inability to communicate what is important; when constantly on the alert and unable to settle.

Description

The plumage of the tūī is iridescent green with purplish-blue and black feathers. Around its neck are white shafted filamentous feathers that curl around the back. Tūī have a white tuff of curled feathers at their throats. Their voices cover a wide frequency range, from bell notes to raucous coughs and melodious song. They can mimic cell phones, backing cars and even the human voice. Tūī play an important role in the ecology of the forest, pollinating plants and disseminating seeds. At communal feeding areas such as kōwhai trees, hierarchies are common, one bird defending a flowering tree or food source against all other birds. They eat nectar, fruit and insects, particularly cicadas and stick insects.

Meaning

This remedy wakes us up. It opens up the chest so that you want to breathe and take in life. It contains a cheeky awareness, a curiosity about what is happening in the world. It opens us to experience joy and defends us from how others might perceive us or influence us with their projections. I see the tūī's love for combat, their feathers flying, wings and beak in the midst of a head-on encounter.

White-faced Heron

Matuku moana
Ardea novaehollandiae novaehollandiae

Essence

Allows the space to dream and not feel compelled to attend to the daily external demands of others; Meditative; the ability to take time to be alone – this aloneness is dream-like and contemplative and has the capacity to balance an organized, busy life.

Use

Use this essence when there is a habit of serving others and allowing no deep quiet, contemplative spaces in life; and for mothers who are constantly running from one job to another. It enables the ability to be solitary in one's endeavours and work. Use when we allow distraction to take us away from what is important in our lives. This essence is particularly helpful in healing soul loss through childhood trauma. It works well in tandem with soul retrieval. It can also be used for children impacted by seeing things in the etheric.

Description

The white-faced heron is a blue-grey bird with a white throat and face and forehead. Its legs and feet are an olive-yellow. It feeds in estuaries, flooded paddocks, rocky shores and sandy beaches. It nests in the crown of tall trees, building a platform of sticks. Foot raking is one of its characteristic hunting methods, striding through the shallows, pausing every two or three metres to stretch out a leg and drag its foot rapidly back and forth to disturb small fish and invertebrates. Often the wings are slightly spread to shade the water surface, increasing the bird's ability to see below the surface.

Meaning

This remedy gives a distinctive awareness of what is happening in the surrounding environment, even the air on your skin. The senses feel extended. It nourishes the inner aspect of the creative rather than focus on the outer aspect of productivity. It allows for understanding the solitary nature of the artist. It allows us to experience dream-like qualities, inward journeying, opening the imaginal mind, fluidity, the ability to become invisible, aloof, alone, experiencing unobtrusive observation. Heron is a companion for the child whose being is not met. It is the child that watches the others and is not able to participate.

Trauma Blends

These blends are the product of collaboration between myself, Leila Lees, and Meggan Young. They have been created due the many enquiries and requests of people who have struggled in various aspects of their lives because of trauma. More people are desiring wholeness and finding courage to live connected to their environment and aligned with spirit. Trauma disrupts this. Through the naming of these blends, the components became clear, each relating to the layered complexity of trauma.

The elemental beings were important in the creation of these remedies. The elemental dimension is not accessed in the world of focus and doing but in the spaces that are around and within. Creating these blends has been commensurate with listening and meeting the elementals, and we have worked in collaboration with these beings. What ensued is a form of alchemy. We recommend that the remedy of choice be taken over time, a few drops three times a day. When taking them, pause and observe what arises.

Remedy for Connection to Life Force

Connecting to life force is like participating in a dynamic field of energy. It is a force. It is the quality which moves you and moves through you. It is, in essence, what excites you, engages you, and enhances you.

This remedy is for those that feel a disconnection to these states and places within themselves. This remedy will support this reconnection. It will allow the person to feel their way back to this connection.

Understanding the connection, and the relationship between it and feeling alive, is vital. When we are cut off from this connection, there can be despair and disparity. Life force makes us visible. Sometimes we give up our life force because of conditioning and to be a part of the world as we think we should be.

The remedy includes the blend of kākā, huia, mulberry, lupin, chickweed, and cleavers essences.

Remedy for Interrupting Negative Thought Patterns

This remedy brings consciousness to our thoughts, to the connection between thoughts and emotions, to thoughts that disrupt action, and to negative thoughts that make you feel stuck and stagnant. Thoughts lead you. Thought comes before form. Thought is part of the creative process. At times thoughts need freedom to wander and create unto themselves. To daydream is to allow the expression of our own mind, to let our thoughts float and wander; this allows them to communicate our fears and desires. This remedy helps us to observe without hooking in with our emotions, to observe as we might observe another without judgment, allowing them to be.

This remedy breaks old patterns of thought, patterns we have created, often to protect ourselves, but now no longer serve us. Often, we hold on to negative thoughts through fear of the unknown. Some people are vulnerable to other people's thinking and become overwhelmed in social situations due to their sensitivity. This essence helps to establish boundaries and helps us to identify what we pick up from others and what we generate ourselves. Dark thoughts of self-judgement and self-hatred can be debilitating as they cycle around, and these repeating negative thoughts are usually a consequence of trauma.

This remedy can also bring in mental sharpness and clarity of mind.

It is made up of a blend of pōhuehue, kōtukutuku, kōtare, diamond, selfheal, and rose quartz essences.

Remedy for Shock

This remedy is for those who have suffered shock and the effects of shock. When we go into shock, the etheric body dilates. People sensitivity is then heightened and they can easily be overwhelmed. This dilation can last for hours or sometimes days and often manifests as a dazed feeling as their etheric body continue to expand and thin out. Shock can cause us to lose faith in ourselves, to falter.

This remedy will support people to pull themselves back together, to anchor in the physical body and feel alive and present. Some shock can be registered in the body and show up years after the event. This remedy enables the body to release the shock gently.

It is made up of a blend of kōtukutuku, kōtare, comfrey, gentian, heron, and clear quartz essences.

Trauma Remedy for Children and Childhood

This remedy supports those that have suffered trauma as a child, trauma locked away until a point in time or a trigger reveals it once again. It can also help to bring a childhood trauma up out of the darkness. As it rises to the surface, we experience a gentle holding enabling us to be present with it for the first time. For adults who focus on their trauma, it will help them let it go, and let it go as part of their identity. We do not need to hold onto these traumas so tightly; a compassionate ear is often all it takes to shift it, whether it is from ourselves or others. So often children may experience powerlessness to control their environment. They become experts at surrendering and making do with what is and what was told to them. This responsibility for our own environment is taken away from us at an early age. Adults often do not know how to allow a child the responsibility and ability to manage and control their environment in positive and intuitive ways that may serve them and be nourishing for them. This can be a trauma in itself.

Children who take this remedy will respond quickly, and in this way, the trauma will not be able to settle. It may dissipate as it moves through the etheric body. We can also work with this remedy alone, sitting quietly with ourselves and observing what bubbles up within a contemplative silence. This remedy would also work with animals.

It is made up of a blend of clematis, sparrow, heron, comfrey, and chickweed essences.

Remedy for the Trauma of Illness

This remedy sustains and supports people to find their way through serious illness. For people suffering from chronic illnesses, it enables them to evolve their relationship with the illness without stagnation or being consumed by it. We should use this remedy when we have lost sight of wellness, leading to despair and overwhelm. It is helpful for people suffering from unknown and undiagnosed illnesses. It brings us back to being present to what is, without leaping ahead to any expected outcome. It helps with the feeling of being in limbo as medical authorities try to eliminate causes. This remedy enables us to feel what personal actions we may take to care for ourselves.

This remedy is also helpful for those who are too focused on the illness and have lost sight of wellness. In the consuming presence of illness, this remedy is like a small hand reaching out. This is wisdom, this hand and your hand, to hold together as you perceive a new outlook, helping to be in relationship with the illness without being consumed by it. There is no force of will in this remedy, rather an ability to be flexible in the face of great constriction.

This remedy works with our aloneness with the illness. It allows for this. This is often what illness requires. Animals go off alone, trusting aloneness with the illness is required. Give space to transition. These are crucial times for a caregiver, the loving one, because they may want to hover and look after you, but they need to listen to the need of the ill person. In the aloneness you sometimes find your alignment, or you get to hear the smaller or quieter voices within, a space away from the thick of people projections.

It is made up of a blend of rose quartz, diamond, cicada, clematis, yarrow, and karamū essences.

Remedy for Creating Space to Exist

Creating a space to exist redefines our sense of self and our wellbeing. The claustrophobic world is a sick world. We all need space to bloom. This remedy will help those to connect to their inner spaciousness and the spaces within their lives. The mind opens to greater intelligence when you consciously connect. The body expands and relaxes with this remedy. Spaciousness is not something we are used to taking up, let alone creating for ourselves. There is so much space within us and around us, and yet we do not consciously connect to it. There is a peace in this state, a willingness to let go and fall into that which is ours for the taking. This is a good remedy for those who feel constricted in their bodies and lives. This remedy is also helpful for children who feel like they don't or shouldn't exist. And for those that struggle to take up space in this world. It will also help elderly people that do not feel they belong or are no longer of value by society. It can help us to understand the underlying elements of our conditioning.

The Space to Exist essence can be taken over a long period of time and has a long term effect. The remedy is not an initiator but an ally, a force that assists. It has the power to help corrode the cages we build around ourselves. The essence needs to be seen within the context of this constriction. But it can only work when the intention or will of the seeker is focused on creating, defining, a space to exist. The essence is also reliant on the seeker's understanding of what constricts them, and will only work within the terms of that understanding. The more deeply the seeker perceives the nature of their constriction, the more powerfully the essence will operate.

This remedy is made from a blend of bee and dandelion essences.